HOCKEY HEROES

Curtis Joseph

KERRY BANKS

GREYSTONE BOOKS
Douglas & McIntyre Publishing Group
Vancouver/Toronto/New York

02 03 04 05   5 4 3 2

Greystone Books
A division of Douglas & McIntyre Ltd.
2323 Quebec Street, Suite 201
Vancouver, British Columbia
Canada V5T 4S7
www.greystonebooks.com

Canadian Cataloguing in Publication Data
Banks, Kerry, 1952–
    Curtis Joseph
    (Hockey heroes)
    ISBN 1-55054-822-0
    1. Joseph, Curtis, 1967– —Juvenile literature.
2. Hockey goalkeepers—Biography—Juvenile literature.
I. Title. II. Series: Hockey heroes (Vancouver, B.C.)
GV848.5.J68B36 2001   j796.962'092   C00-911471-8

Editing by Lucy Kenward
Cover and text design by Peter Cocking
Front cover photograph by Claus Andersen/Bruce Bennett Studios
Printed and bound in Hong Kong by C&C Offset Printing Co. Ltd.
Printed on acid-free paper ∞

The publisher gratefully acknowledges the assistance of the Canada Council
for the Arts and of the British Columbia Ministry of Tourism, Small
Business and Culture. The publisher also acknowledges the financial
support of the Government of Canada through the Book Publishing Industry
Development Program (BPIDP) for its publishing activities.

Photo credits

Photos by Bruce Bennett Studios:
pp. i, 13, 21: John Giamundo
pp. ii, 10, 25 (left): Bruce Bennett
pp. iv, 34, 36,
39, 43: Claus Andersen
pp. 3, 18: Robert Laberge
p. 4, 6, 25 (right): Jim McIsaac
p. 9: Doug MacMillan
p. 14: Art Foxall
p. 17: Jon Hayt
p. 22: Steve Reyes
p. 26: Wen Roberts
p. 29: Vince Muzik
p. 30, 33: Brian Winkler

Photo on page 40
© NHL Images/Silvia Pecota

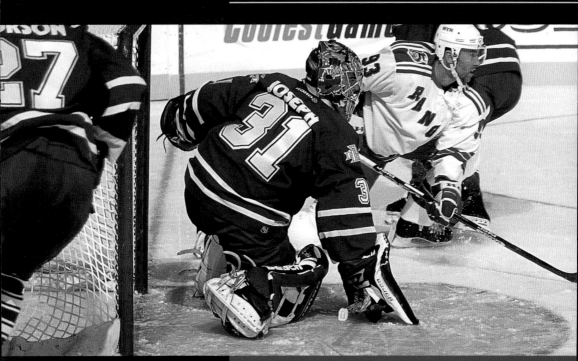

Cool and steady under

fire, Curtis is known for his

ability to inspire his team

by making clutch saves

at key moments.

CHAPTER ONE

The Late Bloomer

The Ottawa Senators were buzzing around the Toronto Maple Leafs zone like angry hornets. It was the opening game of the 2000 National Hockey League NHL playoffs and the Senators looked determined to blow the Leafs out of the Air Canada Centre and into Lake Ontario. But despite several great chances, Ottawa's gunners couldn't beat goalie Curtis Joseph.

During an eight-minute span in the second period, the acrobatic netminder stopped four point-blank shots. Moments later, Darcy Tucker scored to put Toronto up 1–0. One goal was enough. An empty-netter by Mats Sundin completed the 2–0 win. Ottawa's players left the ice dejected. Toronto's masked man had stolen another game. "He was the difference," said Leafs coach Pat Quinn. "I've never seen another goalie who could pick up his team so much with a big save."

The ability to make the big save at the key moment is a Curtis Joseph trademark. No goalie does it more often or in more spectacular fashion. The greater the pressure, the better he plays. As Curtis once noted: "You go out every night hoping to be the difference. That's the mindset you need. You wouldn't want it any other way."

Curtis has displayed this talent not only in Toronto, but also earlier in his career with the St. Louis Blues and the Edmonton Oilers, and with Canada's national team at the 1997 World Championships and the 1996 World Cup. It has helped make him one of the NHL's most highly paid and respected goalies.

Curtis has starred several times in Canada's colors.

Although he's easy-going off the ice, Curtis's personality changes once he straps on the pads. An intense competitor, he doesn't even like it when his teammates score on him in practice. That side of his character is symbolized by his nickame, "Cujo," and his snarling mad-dog mask. Like Cerberus, the three-headed dog of Greek mythology who guarded the gates to hell, Cujo fiercely protects the entrance to the Leafs net.

Blessed with fast hands and feet and amazing flexibility, he plays a reckless, exciting style. Some of his moves look straight

out of street hockey. At times, Curtis may seem off-balance and in trouble, but Leafs backup goalie Glenn Healy insists that's not the case. "There's a method to his madness. He may not play the way the textbooks say, but he has it all figured out."

It is fitting that Curtis should have a unique goaltending style, because everything about his route to the NHL was unusual. Few hockey players have overcome longer odds.

He was born in Keswick, Ontario, in 1967. His parents, Wendy Munro and Curtis Nickle, were just teenagers and not ready to start a family of their own. Four days after his birth, Curtis's mother sadly gave him up for adoption. He was adopted by Jeanne Eakins, a 47-year-old nurse. The little boy was given a name that combined the names of his birth parents: Curtis Munro.

Eakins's two older children had already left home when she adopted Curtis, but she had another adopted son, five-year-old Grant. When Curtis was a toddler, Eakins's marriage ended and the family moved to the nearby town of Gormley, where she married her second husband, Harold Joseph. Curtis's adoptive parents were very strict and often very busy with work. They owned and operated a special-care home for men with mental illnesses.

Because their parents worked such long hours, Curtis
and Grant spent a lot of time alone. To fill the hours they played
sports. They built a long-jump pit in the backyard and a race-
course in the cornfield behind their home. They also played
road hockey in the driveway.

Curtis was usually the goalie. With his older brother firing
shots at him every day, he began to get pretty good. However,
Curtis's mother wouldn't allow him to play hockey on ice—
she thought it was too rough a sport. It wasn't until Curtis was
11 that she finally let him try out for a local house-league
team. The coach put Curtis in goal because he couldn't skate
well enough to keep up with the other boys. Although he was
wobbly on his blades, he had fast reflexes. The other players
couldn't score on him.

The coach told Curtis that if he kept playing he might some-
day become an NHL goalie. That was just what Curtis wanted
to hear. When his mother realized
how badly her son wanted to play,
she got him some equipment and let
him join the team. Curtis practiced
hard. His team, which was in last
place when he arrived, finished the
season in first.

Although he started playing
organized hockey five or six years
later than most Canadian kids,
Curtis developed quickly. He

The Hockey Factory

Notre Dame College, the remote Saskatchewan school where Curtis Joseph
played his last year of junior hockey,
is a remarkable hockey factory. Since it
was founded in 1927 by Father Athol
Murray, more than 50 of Notre Dame's
students have graduated to the
pro ranks. The list includes Wendel
Clark, Russ Courtnall, Gary Leeman,
Gord Kluzak, James Patrick, Rod
Brind'Amour, and Vincent Lecavalier.

had always been very shy, and being good at the sport helped build his confidence and allowed him to make friends.

When Curtis was 17, his parents sold their business and moved to Nova Scotia. He stayed behind and boarded with another family while he attended high school in Newmarket and chased his hockey dreams.

Unlike other players bound for the NHL, Curtis wasn't drafted by a major junior team. Instead, he joined a Tier 2 club: the Richmond Hill Dynes of the Ontario Junior Hockey League. He starred for Richmond Hill for two years and was the league's most valuable player (MVP) in 1986–87. But the Dynes had a poor team and no hockey scouts noticed him. At age 20, in his last year of junior, it seemed as if his career was at a dead end.

Then, Curtis got a lucky break. The local grocer, Paul Sanders, suggested that he apply to the school where his son had played hockey: Notre Dame College in Wilcox, Saskatchewan. To help out, Sanders called the school. Notre Dame was looking for goalies and Curtis was accepted.

Behind his menacing mask, Curtis is a fiery competitor.

Even though Saskatchewan was a long away from Richmond Hill, Curtis made the move. Located about 30 miles (50 kilometers) south of Regina, Wilcox is a tiny town surrounded by empty sky and prairie. Curtis lived with five other players in a trailer. Because he was two years older than anyone else on the team and no longer a high-school student, he worked as a handyman.

It seemed an unlikely place for a goalie to get noticed, but the school had an excellent hockey program. The 1987–88 edition of the Hounds, as the Notre Dame team was known, had several talented players, including Rod Brind'Amour, a future NHLer. Competing that year for the first time in the Saskatchewan Junior Hockey League, the Hounds won the Tier 2 junior national championship. A lot of scouts attended their games. All told, more than a dozen of the club's players earned hockey scholarships to schools in the United States.

Curtis won a scholarship from the University of Wisconsin. The school's hockey team, the Badgers, played in the powerful Western Conference of the National Collegiate Athletic Association (NCAA). The Canadian goalie had a terrific freshman season, leading the Badgers to the quarterfinals of the 1989 NCAA championship. He was voted Rookie of the Year and the conference's MVP, and was second in the voting for the Hobey Baker Award as the top college player in the United States. He wasn't an unknown anymore.

Several NHL teams offered him a contract. Because he had not been drafted as a junior, Curtis was a free agent and could pick the team he wanted to play for. Of all the clubs that approached him, the St. Louis Blues were the most determined.

After discussing things with his agent, Don Meehan, Curtis signed with the Blues on June 16, 1989. The contract was worth US$1.1 million over four years. It was a thrilling moment. Curtis Joseph, the long-shot kid, had just earned a ticket to the big time.

THE CURTIS JOSEPH FILE

Position: Goaltender

Born: April 29, 1967, Keswick, Ontario

Height: Five foot ten inches (1.78 meters)

Weight: 185 pounds (84 kilograms)

Catches: Left

Number: 31

Nickname: Cujo

Favorite Food: Chicken wings

Favorite Subject in School: English

Favorite Musical Group:
The Barenaked Ladies

Favorite Actress: Cameron Diaz

Sports Hero: Muhammad Ali

Hobbies: Raising race horses, fishing, golf

After joining the

St. Louis Blues straight

out of college hockey,

Curtis quickly proved that

he had big-league talent.

CHAPTER TWO

Meet Me in St. Louis

In September 1989, Curtis Joseph attended his first pro training camp. He would compete with veteran Greg Millen and two younger players, Vincent Riendeau and Pat Jablonski, for the two available goalie spots. Any chance Curtis had of making the club vanished when he was injured three days into the camp. St. Louis opened the season with Millen and Riendeau in the nets. Curtis was sent to the Blues' minor-league team, the Peoria Rivermen of the International Hockey League.

Curtis spent a couple of months in Peoria, but just before Christmas, St. Louis traded Millen to the Quebec Nordiques for defenseman Jeff Brown. The trade opened up a goaltending spot and the Blues promoted Curtis to the big team. He started his first NHL game on January 2, 1990, against the Edmonton Oilers. Things didn't go well. The Oilers rifled half a dozen pucks past Curtis, defeating the Blues 6–4.

Curtis didn't play again until January 30, when St. Louis traveled to New York for weekend games against the Islanders and the Rangers. On Saturday, he stopped 24 shots as the Blues beat the Islanders 2–1. The next night against the Rangers, Curtis was called upon to replace Riendeau, who had been injured in a goalmouth collision. When he entered the game, New York was ahead 2–0. He blanked the Rangers the rest of the way, as the Blues earned a 2–2 tie. Next day, sportswriters were calling him "Broadway" Curtis.

With Curtis manning the net, the Blues went on a roll and began challenging the Chicago Blackhawks for top spot in the Norris Division. The rookie goalie was unbeaten in seven starts in February. In those seven games he was selected as the first star four times. He was voted the NHL's Player of the Week for February 10–17, when he notched four straight wins with a sparkling 1.31 goals-against average (GAA).

The Blues finished with 83 points, good enough for second place in

In the Zone

Sometimes a goaltender gets on a roll and stops everything, even shots that are deflected or screened. When this occurs, hockey announcers will say a goalie is "in the Zone." Curtis Joseph once tried to describe the sensation. "It's a feeling that's hard to explain. I don't know how I get into the Zone, and I don't want to know how I get into the Zone. It's just that I am seeing the puck and it looks awfully big. The puck just always seems to hit me."

their division and fifth in the conference. Coach Brian Sutter picked Curtis to start against the Toronto Maple Leafs in the first round of the playoffs. Showing no sign of shaky nerves, he backstopped the Blues to victory. They advanced to meet Chicago in the division final.

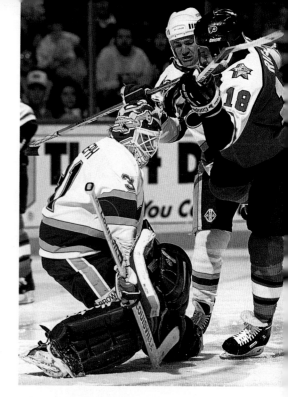

But Curtis didn't start against the Hawks. In the last game of the Leafs' series, he had dislocated his shoulder. With Riendeau between the pipes, St. Louis was eliminated in seven games. It was a disappointing end to the season, but the Blues' performance left reason for hope. They had a young and improving squad. Right-winger Brett Hull led the NHL with 72 goals, center Adam Oates collected 102 points, and Rod Brind'Amour, Curtis's former junior teammate, was one of the league's top rookies.

That summer, Curtis decided to answer a question that had bothered him all his life. By now, he had married his high-school sweetheart, Nancy Dicks, and his adopted mother, Jeanne, had died. With the help of one his stepsisters he made contact with his biological mother. A few years later, he also met his biological father. "I wanted to see where I had come from," he commented later. "It was something that I felt I had to do."

In the off-season, Blues general manager Ron Caron signed free-agent Washington Capitals defenseman Scott Stevens to a contract. Although signing Stevens cost the Blues five first-round draft picks in compensation, Caron felt the sacrifice was worth making to get one of the NHL's top blueliners.

The Blues waged a battle with Chicago for first place in 1990–91, eventually finishing second with 105 points. Hull scored 86 goals, the third-most in league history, while Oates had 90 assists. Riendeau and Joseph both played well, and Sutter was voted the NHL Coach of the Year. But once more an injury cut short Curtis's season. He hurt his knee in late February. By the time it healed, the Blues had been bounced out of the playoffs by the Minnesota North Stars.

Before the start of the 1991–92 season, Caron again dipped into the free-agent market, signing Brendan Shanahan, a star winger from the New Jersey Devils. Because of the signing, the Blues owed the Devils compensation. Caron offered them Curtis and Brind'Amour and two draft picks in exchange. New Jersey's general manager (GM) Lou Lamoriello scoffed at the offer, describing Curtis as "an overpaid, average goalie who is prone to injury." A judge agreed that the Blues' offer wasn't good enough and ordered St. Louis to give up Stevens in return.

Curtis has a unique style of handling the puck.

Curtis learned from the newspapers that he had been offered as trade bait. The news caught him by surprise. He suddenly realized he was expendable. But Curtis's confidence got a boost when the club traded Riendeau to Detroit in October. He was now the team's number-one goalie. Responding to the challenge, he played 60 games in 1991–92, winning 27 of them and recording an impressive .910 save percentage.

But the loss of Stevens, the team captain, was a damaging blow, and the decision to trade Oates to Boston for Craig Janney and Stephane Quintal in mid-season was not a wise move. The Blues slipped to third in the division and fell short in the playoffs, bowing to the Blackhawks in six games. Sutter was fired and was replaced by Bob Plager. Caron said the team was going to change to a swifter, European puck-control style of game.

Slowed by a bad ankle, Curtis got off to a terrible start in 1992–93. As he admitted, "I stink. I just can't seem to make the saves." He was also distracted because the Blues were stalling on giving him a new contract.

The rest of the team wasn't sharp either. It soon became clear that the new puck-control system wasn't working. Plager resigned after 11 games and was replaced by assistant GM Bob Berry, who used a simpler dump-and-chase style. After the coaching change, Curtis's play improved. In February, the club signed him to a new million-dollar contract.

Eager to prove he was worth the money, Curtis competed hard and enjoyed a great year. He played 68 games, led all NHL goalies with a .911 save percentage, and recorded a fourth-best 3.02 GAA. But it was in the 1993 playoffs that the Blues' goalie showed everyone what he could really do.

A RAIN OF RUBBER

During his years in St. Louis, Curtis Joseph was the NHL's busiest netminder. In 1992–93, Curtis played 68 regular-season games and was peppered with 2,202 shots, the most in NHL history at the time. The next year he broke his own record, facing 2,382 shots in 71 games.

Most Shots Faced in a Season

Goalie	Season	Team	GP	Shots
Felix Potvin	1996–97	Leafs	74	2,438
Curtis Joseph	1993–94	Blues	71	2,382
Bill Ranford	1993–94	Oilers	71	2,325
Curtis Joseph	1992–93	Blues	68	2,202

Like all great goalies,

Curtis loves the challenge

of competing in the high-

pressure atmosphere of

the Stanley Cup playoffs.

CHAPTER THREE
Singing the Blues

No one gave the Blues a chance in the 1993 playoffs. They had barely qualified for the postseason, just sneaking in on the last day of the regular season. Even worse, they had to face the mighty Chicago Blackhawks, the best team in the West, in the opening playoff round. But a hot goalie can turn the tide in the playoffs, and St. Louis had a hot keeper.

Curtis slammed the door on the Hawks, recording back-to-back shutouts in Games 2 and 3, as the Blues pulled off a stunning four-game sweep. A surge of playoff fever suddenly swept through St. Louis.

In the division final versus the Maple Leafs, the Blues goalie was even better. In the first two games at Maple Leaf Gardens before a nationwide TV audience, he stole the spotlight. The Leafs dominated play in the first game, outshooting St. Louis 64–34, but barely eked out a 2–1 win in double overtime. Two nights later, Curtis faced 58 shots as the Blues won 2–1 in another double-overtime thriller. In 164 minutes of hockey he had faced 122 shots and allowed only three goals.

An interested observer at the games was former Leafs goalie great Johnny Bower, who remembered Curtis as a teenager when he had attended his goaltending school. "He's got so much confidence right now that he doesn't even feel the pressure of playing in a Stanley Cup game," said Bower.

Back home for Game 3, the Blues stole a 4–3 win, despite being outshot again. When reporters asked Leafs coach Pat Burns to sum up the series so far, he declared in disgust, "It's been Joseph, Joseph, and more Joseph."

Toronto rebounded to win the next two contests, thanks in large part to a new strategy. They screened and interfered with the St. Louis goalie every chance they could. It helped to shake his focus. After a 5–3 loss in the fifth game, Curtis

Out of Nowhere

St. Louis Blues general manager Ron Caron once called Curtis Joseph the "best goaltender to ever come out of nowhere." What Caron meant was that Curtis had reached the NHL despite not being drafted as a junior. Almost every player who makes the NHL is spotted early in his career by a pro scout. Even so, Curtis isn't the only famous puck stopper to slip past the scouts. Eddie "The Eagle" Belfour, the Chicago Blackhawks All-Star goalie that Curtis and the Blues faced in the 1992 and 1993 playoffs, wasn't drafted either.

shaved off his new playoff goatee. "If you don't sleep much, you've got a lot of time to do things like that," he explained.

Clean shaven, Curtis stoned the Leafs 2–1 in Game 6 to send the series to a seventh game. "He's a special kid," remarked Blues coach Bob Berry. "I can't say I'm surprised that he played like he did. He's been doing it for us all year."

But a weary Curtis ran out of miracles in Game 7. The Leafs scored early and often, winning 6–0. Despite the defeat, the Blues' netminder had made a lasting impression with

his supernatural play. He was credited with setting a new mark of excellence for NHL goalies. One reporter went as far as to suggest that "it was as if he was the first guy to run a sub-four-minute mile."

The Blues got off to a fast start in 1993–94. Up front, Hull and Shanahan were having big years and Curtis continued his splendid play, making his first appearance at an NHL All-Star game. He had become one of Missouri's most popular athletes. Blues fans were now calling him Cujo, a nickname created by combining the first two letters of his first and last names. During the 1993–94 season, Curtis introduced a new mask to match his nickname. It featured the face of a snarling dog, just like the rabid St. Bernard named Cujo that terrorized an entire town in a novel by horror writer Stephen King.

Cujo set new team records for most games played (71), wins (36), and shots faced (2,382). But his strong goaltending disguised the Blues' weak defense. A late-season deal to acquire flashy center Petr Nedved from the Vancouver Canucks cost the club two solid defensemen, Jeff Brown and Bret Hedican, further weakening the back line. In the playoffs, the Blues' lack of size and depth on the defense was exposed, as the Dallas Stars rudely swept St. Louis aside in four straight games.

Cujo won a record 36 games for the Blues in 1993–94.

The Blues' swift playoff exit led to some changes after the season. The biggest move was hiring Mike Keenan as the club's new coach and general manager. Keenan, who had just left the

New York Rangers after winning the Stanley Cup, was a successful but controversial coach. Known as Iron Mike, he had a reputation for his harsh methods.

During the lockout-shortened 1994–95 season, Keenan clashed with several of the Blues' star players, including Hull, Shanahan, and Curtis. For whatever reason, Keenan didn't think his goalie had what it takes to be a winner. Several times, the coach criticized Curtis in front of his teammates and pulled him out of games if he didn't think he was playing well enough. "It was hard to go through," Curtis later recalled. "I couldn't imagine anyone treating other human beings that way."

Despite the trouble in the dressing room, the Blues finished second in the Western Conference behind the Detroit Red Wings and Curtis recorded a 2.79 GAA, the best mark of his career. But in the opening playoff round against the Canucks, the Blues goalie was inconsistent. He allowed a couple of soft goals and Keenan twice replaced him with backup keeper Jon Casey in mid-game. When St. Louis lost in seven games, Keenan placed a large part of the blame for the team's defeat on Curtis's poor performance.

Curtis took the criticism hard. As he explained, "Hockey is a game, a kid's game. And I have to be happy to play it." He told his agent that he didn't want to play for Keenan any longer. When the Blues offered him a new contract that summer, Curtis rejected it. On August 4, 1995, St. Louis traded its star goalie to the Edmonton Oilers. His six-year stay with the Blues had ended. He was coming back to Canada.

BEWARE OF THE DOG

Curtis Joseph is known for his interesting and colorful goalie masks. The first one he wore for the St. Louis Blues honored the city's musical tradition. It featured painted trumpets and a scroll of music. In his third season with the Blues, Curtis adopted his famous mad-dog mask. Since then he has had several Cujo masks. The blue-and-white modified cage mask he now wears with the Toronto Maple Leafs is made by Itech and was designed by artist Frank Cipra. Curtis's face peers out from the beast's open jaws. Printed on the back skull pad of the mask are the letters MTT. Those are the initials of Curtis's three children: Madison, Taylor, and Tristan.

In three seasons in

Edmonton, Curtis's charity

work and dazzling play

between the pipes made

him the Oilers' most

popular player.

C H A P T E R   F O U R

Striking Oil

Curtis Joseph's time with the
Edmonton Oilers almost ended
before it started. The goalie and Oilers GM Glen Sather could
not agree on a contract. When talks stalled, Sather re-signed
his other holdout goaltender, veteran Bill Ranford. The move
left Curtis in limbo.

Sather said he would try to trade Curtis but warned it might
take awhile. When nothing was done by November, Curtis
decided to join the Las Vegas Thunder of the International
Hockey League. It was an unusual move, but he felt it would

keep him in shape and put pressure on Sather to make a trade. According to the terms of his deal with the Thunder, Curtis received no salary, but the team paid for his housing, covered his insurance in case he was injured, and provided us$100 a day for expenses.

Curtis was brilliant in Las Vegas. Meanwhile, the Oilers and Ranford were both struggling. By Christmas, Edmonton's playoff hopes were already fading. If Sather had ever intended to trade his holdout goalie, he now changed his mind. On January 11, 1996, Edmonton signed Curtis to a three-year us$6.8-million deal. It made him the team's highest-paid player. That same day, Ranford was traded to the Boston Bruins.

At the news conference to announce his signing, Curtis noted, "Obviously this team has a great tradition of goaltenders. Hopefully I can carry that tradition on." Curtis also revealed that he had bought a luxury suite at the Edmonton Coliseum to be used by children with serious health problems. The box would be called "Cujo's Cloud Nine."

Curtis kept his career on track with the Las Vegas Thunder.

Edmonton didn't ease Curtis into the lineup. He began by playing three games in a row, each in a different city. The first was a home date against the Buffalo Sabres and goalie Dominik Hasek. Showing there were no hard feelings over his holdout, the Edmonton fans greeted Curtis with a standing ovation and chanted "Cujo! Cujo!" after he made some key saves. To complete the celebration the Oilers won 5–4 in overtime.

Curtis won his next game for the Oilers in St. Louis against his old tormentor Mike Keenan, and then made it three in a row with a victory in Dallas against the Stars. But the winning streak didn't last. The Oilers had the NHL's youngest team and the inexperience hurt. They failed to make the playoffs. Still, Curtis was enjoying hockey again. After the season ended, he joined Canada's national team at the World Championships in Vienna, Austria, and helped his country win a silver medal.

In August, Curtis was back on the ice preparing to play for Canada again, this time at the 1996 World Cup. Curtis won the starting job and played in seven of the team's eight games. Facing the best in the world, he was sensational. Although Canada lost the final to the U.S., Curtis was voted Canada's most valuable player.

The Oilers mounted a better effort in 1996–97. Sather had put together a fast and exciting team, but because the Oilers liked to play it wide open, Curtis often had to face a ton of shots.

Curtis appeared in 72 of the club's 82 games, only three games shy of Grant Fuhr's team record. He posted 32 wins, the third-highest total in team history, and he recorded a 2.93 GAA. No other goalie in Oilers history had ever posted an

average under 3.00. At the end of the season, Edmonton fans
voted him the team's MVP and the Oilers' most popular player.

As a result of their seventh-place finish, Edmonton met the
Dallas Stars, the conference's second-place team, in the opening
playoff round. The Stars were expected to win easily, but the
series was a tight, seven-game struggle. The last five games
were all decided by one goal. Curtis shut out the Stars twice in
their own building and was especially impressive in Game 5,
stopping 43 shots to spark the Oilers to a 1–0 victory in double
overtime. But he saved his greatest heroics for Game 7.

With the game tied 3–3 late in the third period, he stopped
the dangerous Mike Modano on a breakaway. Then, 12 minutes
into overtime, he made what some call the save of the decade.
During a scramble near the Edmonton net, the
puck squirted free to Joe Nieuwendyk. He shot
quickly, but the red light didn't go on. With a cat-
quick leap, Curtis lunged across the goal line and
stopped the puck with his glove. Moments later,
Oilers forward Todd Marchant burst down the ice
and put the series-winner past goalie Andy Moog.

Curtis owns the Oilers' mark for career shutouts.

But the overmatched Oilers couldn't produce a second upset.
In the conference semifinals they were knocked off by the
defending Cup champion, Colorado Avalanche, in five games.

The next season, Curtis played in 71 games and posted an
even lower GAA of 2.63. Once more the Oilers finished in
seventh place. This time they met Colorado in the first playoff
round. Again the Oilers defied the odds. Down three games

to one and on the brink of elimination, Edmonton rallied to win three straight and take the series.

Curtis led the way, holding Joe Sakic, Peter Forsberg and the rest of the Avalanche snipers off the scoresheet in Games 6 and 7. Afterwards Cujo was mobbed, first by his teammates, then later by reporters hoping to get a quote. "I've never had so many people watch me undress," he joked, as he removed his pads.

Next up were the Dallas Stars. Describing the goalie his team was about to face, Modano said: "He seems to thrive on the moment as well as Patrick Roy. Put Curtis in the limelight like this and as magnified as these games and series are, he seems to step up and make the big save."

But this year, the Stars had their own hot goaltender, Ed Belfour. Dallas got its revenge, winning the series in six hard-fought games. As he skated off the Edmonton Coliseum ice after Game 6, Curtis waved to the fans. No one realized it was his last appearance in an Oilers uniform.

THE PUCK STOPS HERE

Some believe that Curtis Joseph's most dazzling goaltending display occurred on December 10, 1996. That night Cujo made 52 saves for the Edmonton Oilers in a 0–0 draw with the Detroit Red Wings. Afterwards, Detroit center Igor Larionov said, "Joseph was unbelievable. Best I have ever seen anybody play. We try to go five-hole, upstairs, downstairs. He stops them all."

Considering that Larionov had played with legendary Soviet goalie Vladislav Tretiak, that was saying a lot.

Asked by reporters if this was his best shutout, Curtis laughed. "I don't know. It's definitely in the top 10, anyway." Reporters who bothered to check would have discovered that he'd only had nine shutouts in his career to that point.

In his first season with

the Maple Leafs, Curtis's

brilliant goaltending

transformed Toronto into

a Cup contender.

CHAPTER FIVE

Maple Leaf Marvel

Glen Sather wanted to re-sign Curtis Joseph, but the Oilers could not afford to keep him. When his contract expired on July 1, 1998, Curtis became an unrestricted free agent. The Philadelphia Flyers and New York Rangers showed interest, but when they both chose to sign other goalies, the Toronto Maple Leafs entered the picture.

According to Leafs president, Ken Dryden, it was a chance meeting with Curtis's agent in a Toronto variety store that set things in motion. Meehan told Dryden that Joseph was the best

goalie in the league and a positive force in the dressing room, a real leader. "I went into the store only thinking about ice cream," Dryden later recalled, "and I came out thinking that Joseph could be the final piece to make the Maple Leafs a contender for the Stanley Cup."

Although it makes a good story, it's hard to believe that Dryden really thought the Leafs were close to being a Cup threat. The year before Toronto had finished last in its division and 20th overall in the NHL. But Dryden was rebuilding the team. He had just hired a new coach, Pat Quinn, and he had the money to buy new talent. Associate GM Mike Smith and Quinn agreed that Curtis could be a valuable addition.

On July 15, Curtis inked a four-year, US$24-million contract with Toronto. The signing was a shock not only because of the huge dollars involved but because Toronto already had a high-profile goalkeeper: Felix Potvin, who was making US$2.7 million a year.

When Curtis got almost all of the starts early in the season, it was clear that Potvin was on his way out. In December, the upset goalie left the team and was suspended. In January, Potvin was dealt to the New York Islanders for defenseman Bryan Berard.

Curtis didn't let the controversy affect him. Happy to be back in the area where he was raised, he quickly proved his worth. Even when the Leafs were outplayed, he gave them a chance to win. As captain Mats Sundin noted, "It seems the tighter the game gets, the better he plays. When the game gets close he's not letting anything in."

Curtis's skills were well matched to the type of free-wheeling team that Quinn and Smith wanted. Because he was so steady and could handle a lot of shots, Toronto's forwards could play a more aggressive offensive game. If they got caught up ice, they knew their goalie could bail them out. By the end of the season, the Leafs had scored a league-high 268 goals.

In February, the team left its historic home, Maple Leaf Gardens, and moved into the Air Canada Centre. In its last game in the 68-year-old arena, Toronto lost to Chicago, 6–2. It was one of the few things that didn't go right for the Leafs in 1998–99. Paced by Curtis's 35 wins, second-best among NHL goalies, the team had a breakthrough season, improving 28 points over the previous year and placing third in the Eastern Conference. For the first time since 1995–96 Toronto was in the playoffs.

In the opening round, Toronto met the Philadelphia Flyers, a crew of tough, brawny players. As expected it was a physical series.

Keeping Cool

Curtis Joseph is known for his acrobatic netminding, but he also excels at the mental part of the game. As Toronto Maple Leafs goalie Glenn Healy notes, "Your mind is a real asset when you're playing goal. You have to be able to keep cool no matter what is sent your way. Curtis's mental approach is essential to his success. Nothing seems to faze him. He's unflappable."

And like so many series, it was eventually decided by goaltending. Curtis outplayed John Vanbiesbrouck, the goalie that the Flyers had signed instead of him back in the summer. Despite scoring only nine goals, an all-time low for a winning team in a six-game series, the Leafs prevailed. They clinched their victory with a 1–0 cliffhanger on Philly ice.

"I don't know how many times it looked like we had him beaten, and the Leafs came right down and scored on us," commented the Flyers' Eric Lindros. "That kind of goaltending can really take the air out of you."

After beating the Flyers, the Leafs defeated Jaromir Jagr and the Pittsburgh Penguins to advance to the Eastern Conference final with the Buffalo Sabres. But with that series tied at one game each, the Sabres raised their game. A tired-looking Leafs team went down in five games. Although Toronto fans didn't like the way the storybook season had ended, they couldn't complain too much. The club had come a long way in one year.

During the off-season, associate GM Mike Smith left the club in a dispute with Dryden, and Quinn added the GM job to his coach's title. Although some felt the Leafs had not done enough to solve their weaknesses over the summer, those worries faded when the club burst out of the starting gate in 1999–2000. A quarter of the way through the schedule, Toronto had the best record in the league.

Although it was still scoring at a fast clip, the club had also improved its defensive play. Cujo's stats reflected the change.

Even in heavy traffic, Cujo never loses sight of the puck.

CUJO'S KIDS

In June 2000, Curtis Joseph won the King Clancy Trophy, an annual award given to the NHL player who makes a noteworthy humanitarian contribution to his community. As part of his contract, Curtis leases a $100,000 luxury suite at Toronto's Air Canada Centre. At each Leafs home game, children suffering from cancer and other serious illnesses use the box. After the game, the Leafs' goalie meets the kids and signs autographs. Curtis also helped sponsor the building of Cujo's Crease, a room at Toronto's Hospital for Sick Children, where kids stay before having surgery. The room is painted to look like the Leafs' dressing room. As well, he hosts an annual Ontario golf celebrity tournament that benefits the Childrens' Wish Foundation.

After 22 games, he had a 1.88 GAA, the best in the NHL. But the Leafs soon reverted to their offensive-minded ways. By the season's end, Curtis was averaging 30 shots a game. Still, his final stats—a 36-20-7 win-loss-tie record and a 2.49 GAA—were even better than the previous year. He was nominated as a finalist for the Vezina Trophy as top goalie.

"He's as much responsible for our development as anyone," declared Quinn. "Last year we had no expectations from our young defense, but Joseph settled everyone down. He was solid as a rock and that has continued."

Despite topping the Northeast Division with 100 points, the Leafs were not favored to win the Cup. Late-season deals for Darcy Tucker and Gerald Diduck had added to the team's toughness, but most hockey experts felt they still needed more. And too, they had lost Bryan Berard, their best puck-carrying defenseman, to a career-ending eye injury.

Toronto's first-round opponent, the Ottawa Senators, pushed the Leafs hard. After losing the first two games, the Senators bounced back with 4–3 and 2–1 wins. But after that Curtis took control. In Game 5, he outduelled Ottawa goalie Tom Barrasso in a 2–1 overtime squeaker, then turned away 36 shots as the boys in blue took the series with a 4–2 win.

Things got tougher in the next round. Fresh off a four-game sweep of the Florida Panthers, the New Jersey Devils came in riding a wave of confidence. The teams split the first two games: the Leafs winning 2–1 and the Devils 1–0. But back at home in Game 3, New Jersey outhit and outshot Toronto, winning 5–1. The Leafs' top scoring line of Mats Sundin, Steve Thomas, and Jonas Hoglund was checked into the ice.

The Devils were just as dominant the next game, but were repeatedly frustrated by the goalie in the dog mask. A narrow 3–2 win put Toronto back in the series. "Thank God we have Cujo," said the Leafs' Tie Domi.

But the Devils were too strong. They posted a 4–3 win in Game 5, then wrapped up the series with a 3–0 victory on home ice. Devils goalie Martin Brodeur never had an easier shutout. The Leafs managed just six shots on net.

Although Quinn and Dryden had greatly improved the team, the task was not finished. Realizing the team needed more muscle and leadership to make the final push for the Stanley Cup, Leafs management signed three veteran free agents before the 2000–01 season: hardrocks Gary Roberts, Shayne Corson, and Dave Manson.

Curtis is a netminder who thrives on plenty of action.

For the Leafs and their star goaltender, the focus is capturing that elusive Cup, last won by a Toronto team in 1967. Getting his hands on Lord Stanley's fabled jug would be the crowning glory on Curtis's career. As he noted, "When you're a young player, you think there will be lots of championships to come. But I know now that it doesn't happen that way, and you have to take advantage of the chances you get."

Maple Leafs fans believe that with Cujo guarding the goal, the chances of the Cup coming to Toronto have never been better.

STATISTICS

Ontario Junior Hockey League

Year	Team	GP	W	L	T	SO	GAA
1985–86	Richmond Hill	33	12	18	0	1	5.45
1986–87	Richmond Hill	30	14	7	6	1	4.35
Totals		63	26	25	6	2	?

Saskatchewan Junior Hockey League

Regular Season

Year	Team	GP	W	L	T	SO	GAA
1987–88	Notre Dame	36	25	4	7	1	2.59

Centennial Cup

Year	Team	GP	W	L	SO	GAA
1988	Notre Dame	5	4	1	0	3.17

National Collegiate Athletic Association

Year	Team	GP	W	L	T	SO	GAA
1988–89	Wisconsin	38	21	11	5	1	2.49

International Hockey League

Year	Team	GP	W	L	T	SO	GAA
1989–90	Peoria	23	10	8	2	0	3.87
1995–96	Las Vegas	15	12	2	1	1	1.99
Totals		38	22	10	3	1	3.09

National Hockey League (NHL)

Regular Season

Year	Team	GP	W	L	T	SO	GAA
1989–90	St. Louis	15	9	5	1	0	3.38
1990–91	St. Louis	30	16	10	2	0	3.12
1991–92	St. Louis	60	27	20	10	2	3.01
1992–93	St. Louis	68	29	28	9	1	3.02
1993–94	St. Louis	71	36	23	11	1	3.10
1994–95	St. Louis	36	20	10	1	1	2.79
1995–96	Edmonton	34	15	16	2	0	3.44
1996–97	Edmonton	72	32	29	9	6	2.93
1997–98	Edmonton	71	29	31	9	8	2.63
1998–99	Toronto	67	35	24	7	3	2.56
1999–00	Toronto	63	36	20	7	4	2.49
2000–01	Toronto	68	33	27	8	6	2.38
Totals		655	317	243	76	32	2.83

Playoffs

Year	Team	GP	W	L	SO	GAA
1990	St. Louis	6	4	1	0	3.30
1992	St. Louis	6	2	4	0	3.64
1993	St. Louis	11	7	4	2	2.27
1994	St. Louis	4	0	4	0	3.66
1995	St. Louis	7	3	3	0	3.67
1997	Edmonton	12	5	7	2	2.82
1998	Edmonton	12	5	7	3	1.93
1999	Toronto	17	9	8	1	2.43
2000	Toronto	12	6	6	1	2.06
2001	Toronto	11	7	4	3	2.10
Totals		98	48	48	12	2.57

Key

GP = Games Played   W = Wins   L = Losses   T = Ties
SO = Shutouts   GAA = Goals Against Average